chagall

chagall

Text and Layout design by
MARIE-THÉRÈSE SOUVERBIE

LEON AMIEL PUBLISHER
NEW YORK

Published by
LEON AMIEL PUBLISHER
NEW YORK, 1975
ISBN 0.8148.0633.3
© 1975 ADAGP
· Printed in Italy

The Grandmother
1922-1923

Marc Chagall appeared in the midst of the upheavals that have marked our century like a strange magician come to reveal the secrets of another world. He was born in Vitebsk in 1887, a town where the Russian soul and Jewish traditions, the source of all his inspiration, mingled and fermented together. Chagall spent his lifetime painting his native country, his people, the humble and the fervent.

I am Your earthly son
I can barely walk
You filled my hands with brushes and colors
But I don't know how to paint You.

Should I paint the sky, the earth, my heart
Burning cities, fleeing people
My streaming eyes
Or should I escape, fly toward whom?

He who generates life here below
He who dispenses death
Perhaps he will see to it
That my picture is illumined...

Marc Chagall, poems 1940-1945

Self-Portrait
at the family
1922-1923

As early as the age of eight Chagall knew he would be painter, even though there was no precedent for this vocation in his family. A painter from Vitebsky, Pen, accepted him in his studio; then, in 1907, Chagall attended the Academy of the Arts in Saint-Petersburg. But the courses he took there were dull and had little to offer, and it was not until Chagall entered Bask's "New School" that he discovered modern art. However, the decorative experiments of this group did not really touch him. What he did discover was the autonomous value of color and of linear distortion. His art was already marked by his individuality; he painted themes of birth, life and death, as well as portraits of Bella, the woman who played such an important role in his life.

But it was Paris that attracted him. A friend, deputy of the Douma, agreed to finance his trip there. He thus discovered in 1910 the special light of Paris, which for him was equivalent to the light of freedom he had already dreamed of. In the ateliers of Montparnasse, at the Grande Chaumière, at the "Ruche" where he settled, he discovered a thriving, at once cosmopolitan and bohemian life. He met Modigliani, Soutine, Delaunay, La Fresnaye, and the Cubists, and participated with them in the creation of a new form of Western art.

The poets who were grouped around Blaise Cendrars and Apollinaire adopted him immediately as one of their own, fascinated by the

Etching for Gogol's "Dead Souls" 1923

unusual world he brought to life in his pictures. Didn't Chagall also desire "to break the joints of the world," as Aragon put it? "Hey! I think it's my own head that's hanging desolately in space," wrote Blaise Cendrars, who gave strange titles to the pictures of his friend, such as *To Russia, Asses,* and *Others, Anywhere out of the World, The Poet or Half Past Three*. Many of Apollinaire's poems, such as "Through Europe or Rodztag," were inspired by Chagall's personality. What united these artists and writers was their belief that realism was dead. But they did not remain together for long; André Breton, the leader of Surrealism, in particular distrusted the "mystical" aspect of Chagall's inspiration.

An exhibition was then organized in Berlin by Walden, a friend of Apollinaire's, at the "Der Sturm" Gallery. It had considerable impact and greatly influenced the German Expressionist movement just before the war of 1914.

The pictures dating from this period show Cubist influences, such as the *Landscape of 1918* or *Self-Portrait with Seven Fingers*, but whereas the Cubists imprisoned forms within a geometrical universes, Chagall sought to liberate reality in order better to express the vision of his inner world. The various objects that he threw helter-skelter on his pictures—clocks, crucifixes, chandeliers, bestiaries—were no more than the expression of a certain humor with regard to subsidiary elements.

It would be hard to think of another painter

Self-Portrait at the Easel 1922-1923

whose spirit is more unconventional than Chagall's. He did not allow himself to be absorbed by Cubism any more than he did by Surrealism. In the last analysis, he remained faithful only to himself and his own vision. ..."I could work tranquilly next to the arrogant Cubists. They didn't bother me. I looked at them from a certain distance and I thought, let them have their fill of their square pears on their triangular tables. My art is irrational, a flamboyant go-between, a blue spirit springing out of my pictures. And I thought, down with realistic naturalism, Impressionism, and Cubism, they make me feel sad and constrained. What kind of an epoch is this that sings hymns to technology and worships formalism? Let my madness be welcome, let it be an expiatory train, a revolution of content and not of form." Chagall even went so far as to think of formalism in terms of the pope in Rome "sumptuously clothed next to the naked Christ."

Chagall's freedom finally made him very solitary. For just as Chagall avoided conventions, he avoided being included in groups, schools or ideological systems. His work tells us about his life, and he undertook not only to relate his life but to reveal and explore its deeper meanings.

Returning to Russia when war broke out, Chagall was mobilized (affected to camouflage). In 1917, after the revolution, he was named Commissar of Fine Arts at Vitebsk. He im-

Man with Sentinel
1925-1926

mediately called upon Lissitzky, Pougny and Malevich to organize an academy where all the trends of modern art would be represented, but their association did not last long. Nor were Chagall's initiatives always looked upon with a friendly eye by the local authorities. "I accepted craftsmen in my school," Chagall said, "painters who knew their craft better than I. We were commissioned to do projects or else we competed in the communal ateliers. We tried to bring art closer to life... We decorated houses, tramways, trains. But the officials failed to understand why we painted blue cows on houses to celebrate the revolution, instead of

The Lovers Above the Town. Lithograph. 1921-1923

making portraits of Marx or Lenin." Chagall reacted with humor to these reproaches. He painted a picture portraying Lenin as an acrobat, upside down, his feet in the air, his hands flat on a table, in the midst of a meeting. Revolutionaries waved banners while the common people went about their daily occupations.

Chagall resigned from his post and returned to Moscow where Granovsky had commissioned him to decorate the Jewish theater. Chagall had already worked for the theater, having designed sets for plays by Gogol and Synge, but his convictions had too little in common with those of the directors, with Stanislavsky's "theater of style." It was with Meyerhold, at the Jewish theater, that he was able to achieve a harmonious collaboration between the director, the designer and the actors, resulting in a collective performance. It was a question of creating a magical ambiance in which mobile elements like light and color would truly play their role in the same way as the text and the actors. Scenic conventions, effects of perspective, historical or folkloric reconstructions were eliminated; the drama was more evoked than it was clearly defined. In order to increase audience participation, Chagall even decorated the walls of the theater. Large frescoes suggested music, dance and literature by means of cubist figures, whereas the world of the theater—musicians, playwrights, acrobats, actors—was rendered by a highly animated composition in which figures stood out against a background made up of dynamic diagonals and curves.

Chagall's fondness for music, dance and entertainment runs like a leitmotif throughout his life. His influence in these fields has been considerable.

In 1922 Chagall obtained an exit visa to exhibit in Berlin, where he settled with his wife Bella and his daughter Ida. It was in Berlin that he wrote his autobiography "My Life" which he illustrated with en gravings. On both an intellectual and material level, Germany was the ideal place to produce prints. Chagall learned the different techniques of etching, drypoint

and woodcut in the Sturk workshop. Chagall
was also able to see the work of the German
Expressionists, especially of Grosz.

Vollard, in Paris, was fascinated by the spon-
taneous and subtle qualities of Chagall's engravings, and he invited Chagall to work with him.
Thus began a long and fruitful collaboration
that only came to an end with Vollard's death
during the war of 1939-1940. Vollard first
commissioned the artist to illustrate Gogol's
"Dead Souls." The result was successful, un-
doubtedly because of the close relationship
between the text and the work Chagall was doing
at the time in which he sought to bring the
spirit of old Russia to life. Chagall used a fine
and sinuous line to evoke the setting of Gogol's
story, the characters and their attitudes.

To illustrate La Fontaine's *Fables*, Chagall
did more than a hundred gouaches directly from
nature. "I plunged into these new themes that
were so different from anything I had ever seen
in Vitebsk... flowers from the south of France,
Savoy peasants, well-fed animals. After the
Revolution, hunger and poverty, I gave free
rein to my appetite." In Chagall's fabulous
world, the boundary line between men and
animals is very indistinct, which perhaps accounts
for the strangeness and wonder we feel when
we enter it.

It was not easy to achieve the technical mastery
necessary to express the areas of shadow and
light Chagall desired to evoke. But Chagall's

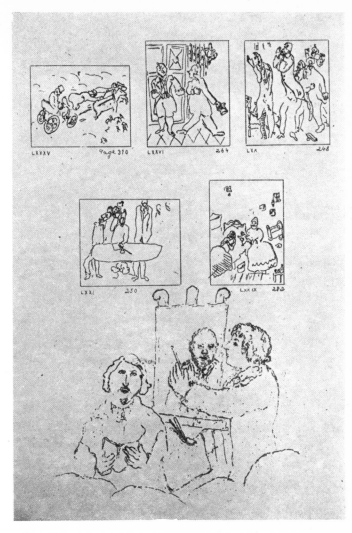

Etching for Gogol's "Dead Souls". 1923

The Horse Who Wanted
Revenge on the Stag
1928-1931

most important work in the field of engraving
is the Bible. It is in this series of 105 etchings
that he gives us his full measure as an artist.
The *Bible* was the fruit of Chagall's travels in the
Holy Land and of many years of work. The
amount of work involved is evident from the
"technical trituration" of each plate. We can
see how Chagall constantly reworked his themes,

simplifying, polishing them, adding to them. "I'm sure that Rembrandt loves me," he even said.

Chagall's engraved work is very important. Perhaps it reveals even more than his painting the characteristics of his art. The rigor inherent in the technique of the drypoint emphasizes the acuity of his vision, the poetic and tender irony that defines it. Many of the themes that Chagall took up later for the "Biblical Message" are already expressed here.

The outbreak of World War II had a profound effect on Chagall. The style and inspiration of his work changed completely. He painted dramatic visions of the world, such as the *Fall of the Angel*—one of his most beautiful pictures—or crucifixions. During the Nazi occupation of France Chagall took refuge in the United States, where Bella died in 1944. This was the darkest period of his life. Chagall tried to synthesize everything he had loved (and his love for Bella) in large pictures evoking the past and the next world.

Henceforward, color would become increasingly important in Chagall's work as beings and things, divested of their individuality, were merged in a sort of diffuse lyricism, a luminous vibration.

In 1942 Chagall was commissioned to execute the sets and costumes of *Aleko* for the New York Ballet Theater. The choreographer Léonide Massine mounted this work with music by Tchai-

kovsky and a poem by Pushkin, "The Gypsies."
The tragic story of this murderous poet touched
Chagall deeply. He read and reread the text
while listening to the music on a record, and he
painted four large pictures for the stage curtains
which are extraordinarily suggestive funereal
reveries. We see a wheat field ablaze with color
under the mass of two enormous red suns, and
a wild horse (for the second curtain) leaping
into the dark sky above the reddish hue of the
city. These images are unforgettable. The
costumes are typically Chagallian, full of fantasy
and invention, especially those of the hybrid
creatures who are half-human, half-animal. A
little later Chagall designed the sets for Stravinsky's *Firebird*, staged in London at Covent
Garden in 1950. It is interesting to note that
this ballet was performed for the first time by the
troupe of the Ballets Russes in 1915. In this
work Chagall gave color a major role. The three
acts are as if bathed in a sombre atmosphere of
magic and enchantment. The opening curtain
shows a bird soaring into the deep blue night,
carrying a young woman who resembles Bella.
It is difficult to say whether we see the young
woman from above or below on account of the
strange, thrown-back position of her head.

...."I wanted to penetrate the spirit of the *Firebird* and *Aleko*," Chagall said, "without illustrat-
ing them, without copying anything. I'm not
trying to represent anything. I want color to
speak for itself and to act alone."

Eliezer and Rebecca. 1931

When in 1959 Chagall was commissioned to do the sets for Ravel's *Daphnis and Chloe* for the Chicago Opera, he went even further in this direction. To find the visual equivalent for Ravel's music was a challenging problem, and Chagall solved it by indulging freely in his love for the Mediterranean world and creating a kind of vegetable delirium. The sets were bathed in an immaterial atmosphere, a lighting that itself became musical vibration.

When Chagall returned definitively to France in 1947 and settled at Vence in Provence, a new period in his life began. He married Valentine Brodsky (Vava), he was happy and his work by now had achieved international recognition. From this moment on a sort of bacchic jubilation becomes evident in his work, suns are seen bursting out everywhere, and beautiful women are as if submerged in bouquets of flowers and an abundance of fruit. The ram with the golden eyes and the rooster—sexual symbols— are always surging up somewhere in his pictures, and color assumes more and more importance at the expense of form.

In this region where "the land burns your fingertips" he discovered ceramics. Vence was next to Vallauris, the village of potters where Picasso lived. Chagall decorated pieces (exhibited at Maeght's in 1950) and modelled small, charming figurines. Chagall, for whom color was so important, was quickly attracted by the possibilities offered by glaze and the techniques

Jeremiah
Etching for the Bible
1931-1956

of fire. Here color and substance truly became one.

It was also at Maeght's that Chagall met Mourlot, the lithograph printer, in relation to a poster for an exhibition. At Mourlot's workshop he began a new series based on the theme of the Bible and *Daphnis and Chloe*. Chagall described the parodisiac vision of a world without sin, very different from the first series on the Bible he had done for Vollard which suggested the terror one feels when confronted with the Divine.

The Firebird
Drawing
1945

To execute these monumental works, Chagall sought the help of the best artisans, glassmakers, mosaicists, weavers, and ceramists. First he did a ceramic work for the church of the plateau d'Assy, then the stained-glass windows for the Metz Cathedral (executed by André Marc), the twelve windows of the synagogue of the new Hadassah Medical Center in Jerusalem (1962), those of the Union Church at Pocantico Hills in the United States (1970), and those of Rheims (1972). Chagall excelled in animating these huge architectural spaces by means of the play of light through stained-glass.

Chagall's tapestries for the Knesset in Jerusalem were woven at the Gobelins in Paris. These enormous, rather austere works suggest Exodus and the songs of David.

In 1968 the city of Nice commissioned Chagall to decorate a large wall of the new faculty of law. Chagall then designed the cartoon for a mosaic based on the theme of the *Odyssey*. He did another large mosaic for the Biblical Message on the Cimiez Hill in Nice. Elijah the prophet is shown on a fiery chariot in the midst of an allegorical world of figures and animals.

In the meantime, André Malraux had asked Chagall to repaint the ceiling of the Paris Opera. In spite of his seventy-five years of age, Chagall agreed to undertake this considerable task. It was necessary to unite the disparate and excessive elements of the gigantic edifice. Chagall conceived an immense composition animated by colored

Lithograph for the Circus. 1967

volumes and fluid shapes. Although the work he did remains controversial, it succeeds in establishing a feeling of harmony.

In 1967, for the Metropolitan Opera in New York, Chagall did the curtains for Mozart's *The Magic Flute*. Here Chagall dreamed of a total spectacle in which sounds and colors, merging together, would function in total unison. In order to truly express the tonality of Mozart's opera, Chagall reworked the curtains and costumes many times. Seldom, if ever, have artists succeeded in rendering so precisely the correspondences between Mozart's music and color. Chagall may be thought of as a pioneer in this domain.

But henceforward the project closest to Chagall's heart was the execution of the "Biblical Message." A small building was erected on the Cimiez hill above Nice. It was here that a group of pictures dealing with the principal themes of the Bible, Exodus, Genesis, and the Song of Songs, were brought together in order to allow those who would visit this haven of peace "to feel a certain presence." Finally the stained-glass windows and the mosaic were finished, and the Biblical Message was inaugurated in 1973.

Although Chagall has drawn much of his inspiration from the Bible, it cannot be said that he is truly a religious painter. Here also it is difficult to fit Chagall into a definite category. In a way, there is something provocative about his vision of the sacred. His characters seem to

Nous voulons le
Bonheur
Teinté de couleurs
claires

Libre des Tumultes de
La Terre. Ainsi cette Forme
d'art Pourrait
entrer au paradis
comme y est parvenue
La Flute enchantée
de Mozart.

Marc Chagall

develop with total freedom of movement and feeling. As Chagall puts it, "I have always thought of actors, clowns and acrobats as tragically human beings who resemble the characters we see in certain religious paintings."

The two themes of the Bible and the circus constitute the main axes of his work and they develop in genuine cycles. Chagall's fascination with the circus dates from the gypsy spectacles he saw in his childhood, but he also was fond of going with Vollard to the Cirque d'Hiver. It is difficult to imagine today the artistic importance of the shows created by great artists like the Fratellini, Grock or Chocolat. "For myself," says Chagall, "there is something magic about the circus... it's a world in itself... the most intense cry in relation to man's search for amusement or joy often takes on the form of the highest poetry." A curious engraving from the series on the *Circus* (commissioned by Tériade) shows Moses in the center of a circus arena holding the Tables of the Law in his hands, while a fiddler is hanging from his belt, as well as a clock and a crucifix. The point of this is that Chagall's vision of the biblical world is alive and human and not conventional and fixed.

Don't the prophets, like the clowns and the saints, participate in the flux of established values in our world? Gravity does not hold them down; truth lies elsewhere. And if the world seems upside down, it is perhaps we who have lost our sense of direction.

Jonas - Drawing for the Bible. 1958-1959

"Everything can change if we pronounce the word love without shame," declares Chagall. "The true spirit of art resides in love."

As we have seen, Chagall's work exists outside of the main currents of modern art. Chagall's work tells a story, his painting is an autobiography, but that of a poet for whom time and space are not important, and for whom, as in children's paintings, animals and human beings exist on the same level. But this apparent simplicity actually overthrows all the conventional barriers. Chagall is present at the different crossroads that mark the evolution of twentieth-century painting. His authenticity is beyond question. And although his vision seems immutable, Chagall has known how to skillfully adopt the most contemporary researches and to provide his own answer to the problems of our time.

"I'm a child of a certain age," Chagall says. "Each day we're a little bit younger."

Chagall's role, as time goes by, stands out more and more clearly.

Translated by
Wade Stevenson

Composition
1964-1965

BIOGRAPHY

1887
Birth of Marc Chagall at Vitebsk (Russia) on July 7.
1906
Studies at Pen's school of painting.
1907
Leaves for Saint-Petersburg and enters the School of the Royal Academy for the Encouragement of the Arts.
1910
Leaves for Paris. Settles at "la Ruche." Meets Cendrars, Max Jacob, Apollinaire, and the painters Léger, Modigliani, La Fresnaye.
1911
Starting in 1911, he exhibits every year, once at the Salon d'Automne. Friendship with Cendrars.
1914
Apollinaire introduces Chagall to Herwarth Walden who gives him an important exhibition at the Galerie Der Sturm in Berlin. Chagall leaves for Russia.
1915
He marries Bella at Vitebsk. Comes back to Saint Petersburg where he is mobilized.

1917

After the October revolution he returns to Vitebsk. Is appointed Commissar of Fine Arts in the Vitebsk government. Founds the Academy of Fine Arts and invites Lissitzky, Pougny and Malevich as professors.

1919

Chagall resigns. Invited by Effros and Granovsky, he goes to Moscow and executes a series of mural paintings for the auditorium of the new Jewish Theater.

1921

Teaches drawing in a colony of war orphans near Moscow.

1922

Decides to return to France. Comes back by way of Berlin where he in vain tries to find his pictures. Cassirer invites him to make a series of engravings on the autobiographical theme of *My Life*.

1923

Chagall settles in Paris again. Vollard commissions him to illustrate Gogol's *Dead Souls*.

1924

First retrospective exhibition in Paris, Galerie Barbazanges-Hodebert. Meets Jean Paulhan, Jules Supervielle, Malraux and Marcel Arlan.

1926

First exhibition in New York (Reinhart Galleries).

1927

Vollard commissions Chagall to illustrate La Fontaine's *Fables*. He becomes friends with Jacques Maritain and Joseph Delteil.

1929

His autobiography, *My Life*, is translated into French and published in 1931.

1931

Travels to Palestine to prepare a series of engravings on the theme of the Bible.

1933

Retrospective of his works at the Basel Museum.

1936-38

Deeply troubled by the rise of totalitarian governments, Chagall begins to emphasize the dramatic and religious aspects of his work.

1939

Carnegie Prize.

1941

Invited by the Museum of Modern Art in New York, Chagall and his wife settle in the United States. Starting in 1941, he exhibits at the Pierre Matisse Gallery in New York.

1942

Trip to Mexico. Sets and costumes for the ballet Aleko (Tchaikovsky).

1944

Death of Bella.

1945

Sets and costumes for Stravinsky's *Firebird*.

1946

Retrospective exhibition at the Museum of Modern Art in New York and at the Art Institute in Chicago.

1947

Chagall returns to Paris. Retrospective exhibition at the Musée National d'Art Moderne in Paris, then at the Muncipal Museum in Amsterdam and the Tate Gallery in London.

1948

Definitive return to France. First Prize of Engraving at the 25th Venice Biennale.

1950

Settles at Vence. Works on ceramics. Retrospective exhibition at the Zurich Museum and then at the Kunsthalle in Berne.

1951

Exhibition in Israel which Chagall visits for the second time. First sculptures.

1952

Marries Valentine Brodsky. Trip to Greece where he

begins to work on the Illustrations for *Daphnis and Chloe*, published by Tériade.

1953
First retrospective exhibition in Turin at the Madame Palace. Start of the series of pictures on the theme of "Paris."

1954
Second trip to Greece. Exhibition at the Galerie Maeght.

1956
Exhibition at the Kunsthalle of Basel and Berne.

1957
Executes large ceramic *The Crossing of the Red Sea*, two bas-reliefs and two stained-glass windows for the Church of the Plateau d'Assy (Savoy). Exhibition of his engraved work at the Bibliothèque Nationale, Paris.

1958
Trip to Chicago where he lectures at the University. Sets and costumes for Ravel's ballet *Daphnis and Chloe* at the Paris Opera. Models for the stained-glass windows at Metz.

1959
Given the title Doctor Honoris Causa by the University of Glasgow. Retrospective exhibition in Paris, Munich and Hamburg. Honorary member of the American Academy of Arts and Letters. Mural decoration for the foyer of the Frankfurt Theater.

1964
Trip to New York. Stained-glass windows for the memorial to Dag Hammarskjöld at the United Nations headquarters in New York, as wells as for the church at Pocantico Hills. The ceiling he painted for the Paris Opera is inaugurated in the autumn.

1965
Doctor Honoris Causa of the University of Notre-Dame (United States). Mural decorations for the new Metropolitan Opera in New York. Sets and costumes for Mozart's *The Magic Flute* in New York.

1966
Settles at Saint-Paul, near Nice.

1967
Retrospectives in Zurich and Cologne for his eightieth birthday. Exhibition of the Biblical Message at the Louvre Museum. Homage at the Fondation Maeght, Saint-Paul. Exhibition "Chagall and the Theater" at Toulouse.

1968
Trip to Washington. Exhibition at the Pierre Matisse Gallery in New York. Mosaic for the U.E.R. Faculty of Law and Economics in Nice.

1969
Places the first stone for the donation of the "Biblical Message" in Nice. Trip to Israel for the inauguration of the Gobelins tapestries at the Knesset in Jerusalem.

1970
Inauguration of the stained-glass windows for the Fraumunster Church in Zurich. Homage to Chagall at the Grand Palais, Paris.

1972
Start of the execution of a large mosaic for the First National City Bank, Chicago.

1973
Inauguration of the Musée National du Message Biblique Marc Chagall in Nice on July 7. Preparation of the model of the stained-glass windows intended for the Rheims Cathedral.

1974
Inauguration of the stained-glass windows at the Rheims Cathedral. First temporary exhibition at the Musée Chagall in Nice.

LIST OF PLATES

PLANCHES

PLATES

1
Nature morte
à la lampe
1910
Still Life with Lamp

2
Le sabbat
1910
The Sabbath

4
La sœur de l'artiste
1909
The Artist's Sister

5
La noce
1909
The Wedding

6
Purim
1916-1918

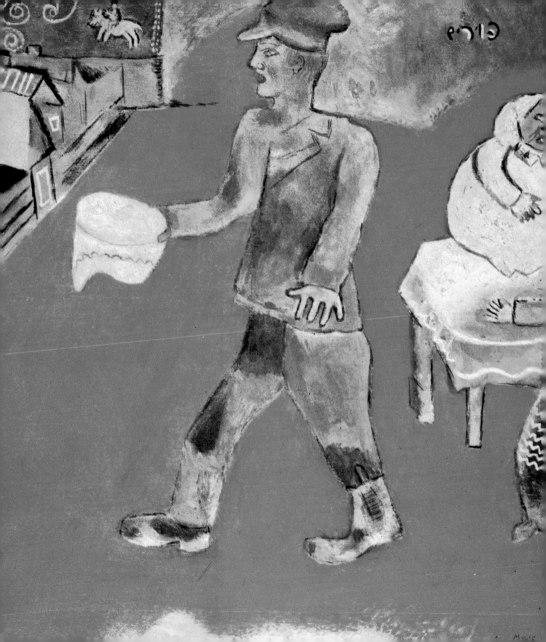

7-8
A la Russie, aux ânes, aux autres
détail et ensemble
1911
To Russia, Asses and Others

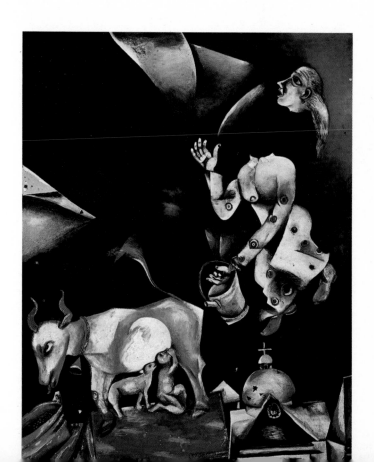

9
Le buveur
1911
The Drunkard

10
Autoportrait aux sept doigts
1912
Self-Portrait with Seven Fingers

11
Le soldat boit
1912
The Soldier Drinks

12
Ma fiancée aux gants noirs
1909
My Fiancée with Black Gloves

13
Le poète
1911
The Poet

14
Hommage
à Apollinaire
1912-1913
Homage
to Apollinaire

15-16
Le rabbin au citron ou jour de fête
ensemble et détail
1914
Feast Day

17
La maison qui brûle
1913
The Burning House

18
Le violoniste
1911
The Fiddler

19
Paris par la fenêtre
1913
Paris from the Window

Esquisse pour le théâtre juif de Moscou
detail
1919
Sketch for the Wall of the Moscow Jewish Theater

20
Au-dessus de Vitebsk
1914
Over Vitebsk

22
La maison grise
1917
The Gray House

23
Le violoniste vert
1923
The Green Violonist

24
L'anniversaire
1915-1923
The Birthday

25
Double portrait
au verre de vin
1917
Double Portrait
with Wineglass

26
La femme enceinte
1913
The Pregnant Woman

27
Le poète allongé
1915
The Reclining Poet

28

N'importe où hors du monde. 1919. Anywhere out of the World

29
Paysage cubiste
1918
Cubist Landscape

30
Les fleurs rouges
1926
The Red Flowers

31
Portrait de Bella à l'œillet
1925
Bella with a Carnation

32
Femme et porcs
1926
Woman and Pigs

33
Homme à la poule
1922
Russian Peasant
with Chicken

34
La mariée à double face
1927
The Bride with a Double Face

35
Jeune fille au cheval
1929
Girl on Horseback

36
La chute de l'ange
1923-1947
The Falling Angel

38
L'arc en ciel, signe d'alliance
entre Dieu et la terre
1931
The Rainbow

39
La cavalière
1931
Equestrienne

40
La jeune acrobate
1926-1927
The Young Acrobat

42
Esquisse pour la révolution
1937
Sketch for the Revolution

43
Le crépuscule
1938-1943
Dusk

45 ▶
Le temps n'a pas de rives
1930-1939
Times is a River Without Banks

46 ▶
Le songe d'une nuit d'été
1939
Midsummer Night's Dream

44
Les mariés de la
Tour Eiffel
1938
Bride and Groom of the
Eiffel Tower

47
Le porteur d'eau.
Esquisse pour le ballet
de l'oiseau de feu
1945
The Water Carrier.
Sketch of Costume
for the Ballet Firebird

Bohémiens. Esquisse pour le ballet Aleko. 1942
Sketch of Gypsies Costumes for the Ballet Aleko

49
Esquisse pour le ballet Aleko
1942
Sketch of Costumes for the Ballet Aleko

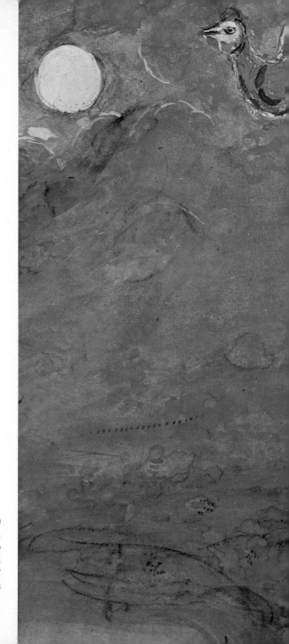

50
Aquarelle pour le premier rideau
du ballet Aleko
detail
1942
Aleko First Curtain

51
La maison à l'œil vert
detail
1944
The House with the Green Eye

52
La nuit verte
1948
The Green Night

53
Obsession
1943

54
L'âme de la cité
1945
The Soul of the City

56
Les toits rouges
1953
Red Roofs

57
Le cirque bleu
1950
Blue Circus

58
L'âne bleu. Céramique. 1954
The Blue Donkey. Ceramic

59
Les trois cyclistes
1957
Trick Cyclists

60
Femme et âne
1943
Woman with a Donkey

61
Hymen. Lithographie pour
Daphnis et Chloé de Longus
1961
Hymenaeus. Lithograph
for Daphnis and Chloe by Longus

62
Joueur de flûte
1954
The Flute Player

63
Le cantique des cantiques
détail
1957
The Song of Songs

64 ▶
Plafond de l'Opéra, Paris
détail
1964
Ceiling of the Opera, Paris
(Photo Jean Dubout)

67
Couple - céramique peinte
1954
Couple - Decorated Vase

68
Environs de Vence
1957
The Neighborhood of Vence

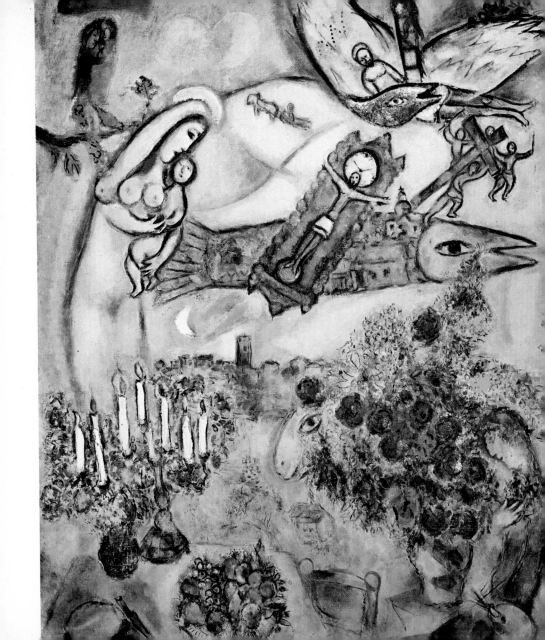

69
Plat en céramique décoré
1950
Ceramic Plate

73
Légende d'Ulysse
détail
1968
Ulysses

75   Le Sacrifice d'Abraham   Lutte de Jacob avec l'ange
       Abraham's Offering   Jacob's Wrestling with the Angel

Le Songe de Jacob
Jacob's Dream

Moïse devant le buisson ardent
Moses Faces the Burning Bush

76
La tribu de Joseph
détail
1961
The Tribe of Joseph

77
La famille d'arlequins
détail
1970
The Family of Harlequins

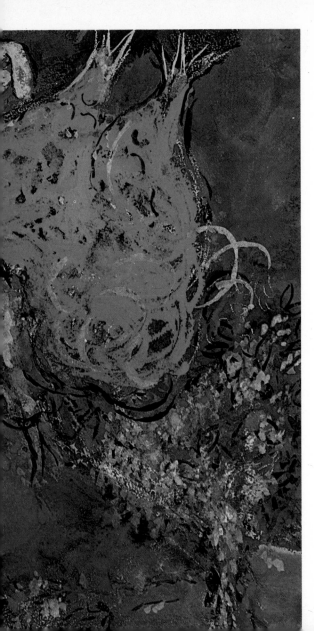

78
Le prophète Jeremie
The Prophet Jeremiah

79-80
L'exode
détails
1964
The Exodus

81-82
Tapisserie du message biblique de Nice
détails
1971
Tapestry of the Biblical Message in Nice

83-84
Etude pour des vitraux
de la Cathédrale de Reims
détail
1972
Study of Stained-Glasses for
the Choir of the
Rheims Cathedral

85
Portrait de Chagall à Nice
1968
Portrait of Chagall in Nice
(Photo André Villers)